WDS
W9-BZU-455

PIGS

A TRUE BOOK

by

Sara Swan Miller

Children's Press®
A Division of Grolier Publishing
New York London Hong Kong Sydney
Danbury, Connecticut

A mud bath

Reading Consultant
Linda Cornwell
Coordinator of School Quality and Professional Improvement
Indiana State Teachers Association

Content Consultant
Jan Jenner

Visit Children's Press® on the Internet at:
http://publishing.grolier.com

Library of Congress Cataloging-in-Publication Data

Miller, Sara Swan.
Pigs / by Sara Swan Miller.
p. cm. — (A True book)
Includes bibliographical references (p.) and index.
Summary: Describes the physical traits, lifestyle, and behavior of pigs and their role in providing humans with meat.
ISBN 0-516-21579-5 (lib. binding) 0-516-27183-0 (pbk.)
1. Swine Juvenile literature. [1. Pigs] I. Title. II. Series.
SF395. 5 .M55 2000
636. 4—dc21

99-30129
CIP

Printed in the United States of America.
1 2 3 4 5 6 7 8 9 10 R 09 08 07 06 05 04 03 02 01 00

Contents

Piglets on a Connecticut farm share a pan of food.

The Pig Story

Have you ever visited a small farm and seen pigs grunting over their feed trough? The pork and bacon found in stores comes from pigs raised on huge factory farms. But many people still raise their own pigs. Why? Isn't it easier just to buy pork from the store?

Pigs are herded on this factory farm in North Carolina.

There's a simple reason. Home-raised pigs make much better-tasting meat.

For thousands of years people hunted wild pigs for their meat. Then about eight thousand years ago people

An ancient boar-hunting scene

tamed them. They began to raise them on their own farms. It was a lot easier than hunting them all over the forest!

Muslims and most Jews don't eat pork. But it's still the most popular meat in the world, especially in Asia. Pork became so popular that the explorer Christopher Columbus

Christopher Columbus brought pigs to the Americas.

brought pigs to islands off the coast of Central America on his second voyage in 1493.

Over the years, people bred the best males with the best females to get the best piglets.

Farmers use skill and hard work to raise the biggest, healthiest pigs.

These Yorkshire-Duroc piglets are crossbreeds.

They wanted the tamest pigs with a lot of tasty meat. They also wanted pigs that had a lot of piglets and were good mothers. Now there are more then fifty breeds, or kinds, to choose from.

Most pigs raised for market are crossbreeds. A male of one breed is mated with a female of another breed. Crossbreeds grow faster, have more young at one time, and stay healthier than purebreds.

A Yorkshire piglet

Some Favorite Pig Breeds

Yorkshires are long and big. They have a lot of piglets at a time. Yorkshire females are known for being good mothers. They get sunburned easily, though. Sometimes farmers have to put sunblock on them!

A Duroc female, or sow

Durocs grow quickly. They need less food than other breeds, but remain heavy. They're hearty and don't get sick easily.

Hampshires are small and lean, but meaty. They're raised for their extra-good meat.

Chester Whites also have good meat. They have a lot of piglets at once and are excellent mothers.

A Chester White pig

Berkshires were brought to the United States from England in the 1840s. They grow quickly and produce especially tasty ham and bacon.

A Berkshire pig

Pet Pigs

Some people keep pigs as pets. Vietnamese potbellied pig were brought to the United States from Asia in 1985. They are very popular.

Potbellied pigs are small, clean, and very smart. They are easily house-broken, and they can learn a lot of tricks. They can learn to play a pig version of soccer, jump through a hoop, and even ride a skateboard.

Caring for potbellied pigs can be fun.

People who love potbellied pigs say the pigs are a lot of fun and very affectionate. They love snuggling up to people and getting a good scratch on their belly.

A pig and its owner take time for a belly rub.

What Are Pigs Like?

A full-grown pig is a big, strong animal. But the pigs raised on small farms are gentle and friendly. They love to have their ears, back, and belly scratched. They will even let young children ride them!

What do you think these pigs are waiting for?

Pigs are smart, too. When they see the farmer coming with a pail of milk, they will run squealing to the fence. They are always on the look-out for a way to escape from their pen.

Pigs have strong, tough snouts and sharp hooves. They sniff and dig in the ground for roots and other good food. But these strong

A pig's nose, or snout, is perfectly shaped for finding food underground.

animals will also uproot a fence by digging and pushing. Or they may stand against the fence and push it over. Farmers need to put up extra-strong fences for pigs.

Pigs can't stand too much heat or cold. They have no thick fur to keep them warm. They don't sweat enough to cool themselves off. In the winter, they need warm shelter. In summer, they need a lot of shade. They also like a

Mud keeps pigs cool and may help them avoid sunburn.

good mud wallow to keep them cool.

Male pigs are called boars. Females are called sows. They give birth to several piglets, or shoats, at once. They usually have eight to ten. The shoats get milk from two rows of

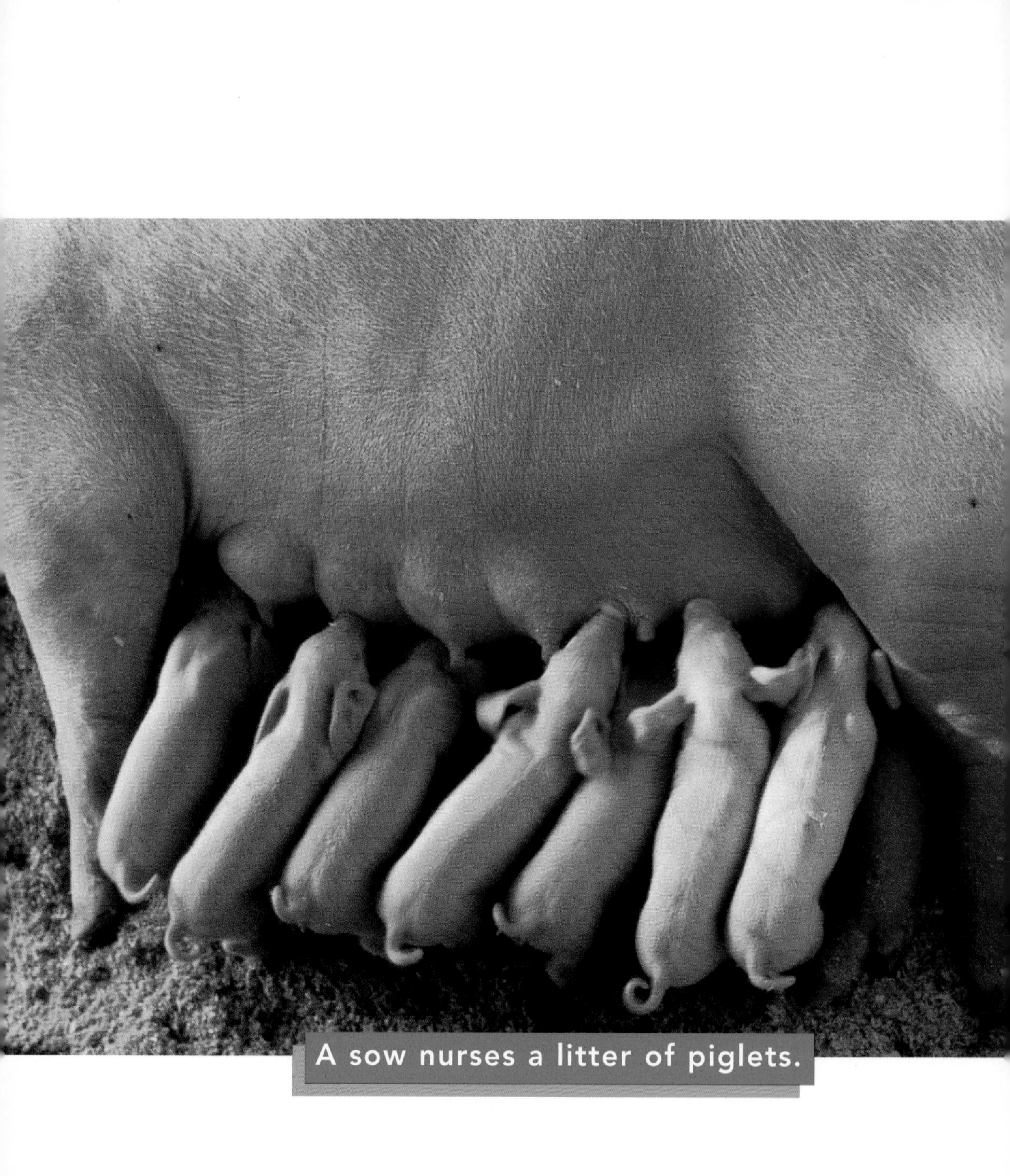

A sow nurses a litter of piglets.

teats on their mother's belly. A sow usually has two litters, or sets, of shoats a year.

The squealing piglets skip about on their toes. They grow quickly. In five and a half months, they weigh about 220 pounds (100 kilograms). Their piglet squeals turn into deep grunts. Then they're called hogs. Hogs keep on growing and growing. The largest hog ever raised weighed more than 1 ton. It

Piglets seem to skip on their toes.

was 9 feet (3 meters) long and 5 feet (2 m) high!

Pigs like eating all kinds of things. In a pasture, they eat roots, grubs, nuts, and plants. In a pen, they eat corn and

These pigs are eating a vegetable chow.

other grains, root vegetables, alfalfa , potatoes, milk, pumpkins, and leftovers from the dinner table. They also like orange juice, potato chips, and candy.

These pigs live on a factory farm.

Pigs on a Small Farm

Pigs that are raised on huge factory farms are usually kept indoors in large buildings. They live in small pens and never have a chance to run around in the sunlight or dig in the ground.

On a small farm, pigs have much more freedom. Many

Pigs root around for food out in the pasture.

farmers let them out in a pasture in the warm months. The farmer gives them small sheds so they can get out of the heat.

Other farmers keep pigs in large pens outside a barn. They make sure the pigs have plenty of space inside and out. Pigs like to be together, but they don't like to be crowded. When they're crowded, pigs don't grow as fast.

Pigs need fresh air, sunshine, and exercise to stay healthy. You can tell a healthy pig by its smooth coat of hair and its bright, alert eyes. Its tail is tightly curled, too.

On a small farm, pigs are kept in pens.

Pigs also need a clean, dry place to sleep. A lot of straw for bedding helps them stay warm. They need a lot of food, too. Farmers make sure their feed troughs are always full.

Pigs of different breeds gather at a feeding trough.

This pig seems to enjoy a cool shower.

When it's too hot, the farmers wet the ground to make a mud wallow. The mud is nice and cool. It keeps the pigs from getting sunburned. Sometimes farmers spray them with a hose. But pigs don't like being wet all the time. They need dry places in their pen and inside the barn.

Some farmers keep sows all year and raise piglets to sell. But a family farm doesn't need twenty new pigs a year. Usually, family farmers buy young pigs from farmers who have sows. These young pigs are called feeders. In the spring, the feeders weigh about 30 to 50 pounds (14 to 23 kg). By late fall they weigh about 200 to 240 pounds (91 to 109 kg). It's time to take them to be turned into meat.

Farmers feed growing pigs as much as they can eat.

Raising pigs is easier than raising cows. For one thing, pigs don't need to be milked. But farmers still have to make sure they stay healthy. They have to clean the pens every day, too. Pig manure, or waste,

A farmer spreads manure in the fields.

is smelly. But it's good for making plants grow. Farmers spread the manure on their crops.

A farm family can get all the meat it needs from two hogs. It does take extra work, but it's worth it. Homegrown pork tastes better than any store-bought pork.

What We Get from Pigs

When you think of pigs, do you think of pork chops and bacon? We get many more things from them than that. They give us ham, roasts, spare ribs, and sausage. Salami and pepperoni are also made from pork. People sometimes eat the tongues

Pork products are sold at this market in Spain.

and the feet, too. They may also make a mixture called scrapple from all the extra bits of meat. First, they grind the bits together. Then corn-meal is mixed in. Then it's cooked in broth.

People all over the world enjoy food made from pigs. Try looking up "pork" in a cookbook. You will be surprised at how many different dishes can be made from pork.

Surprises from Pigs

Can you think of other things we get from pigs? Canned meat, gelatin, and leather are made from pigs. So are glue, fertilizer, antifreeze, and some pet food. A special medicine called insulin comes from pigs. Here's a surprise—soap, makeup, and chewing gum are all made from pigs!

Take a look around your house. How many things can you find that come from pigs?

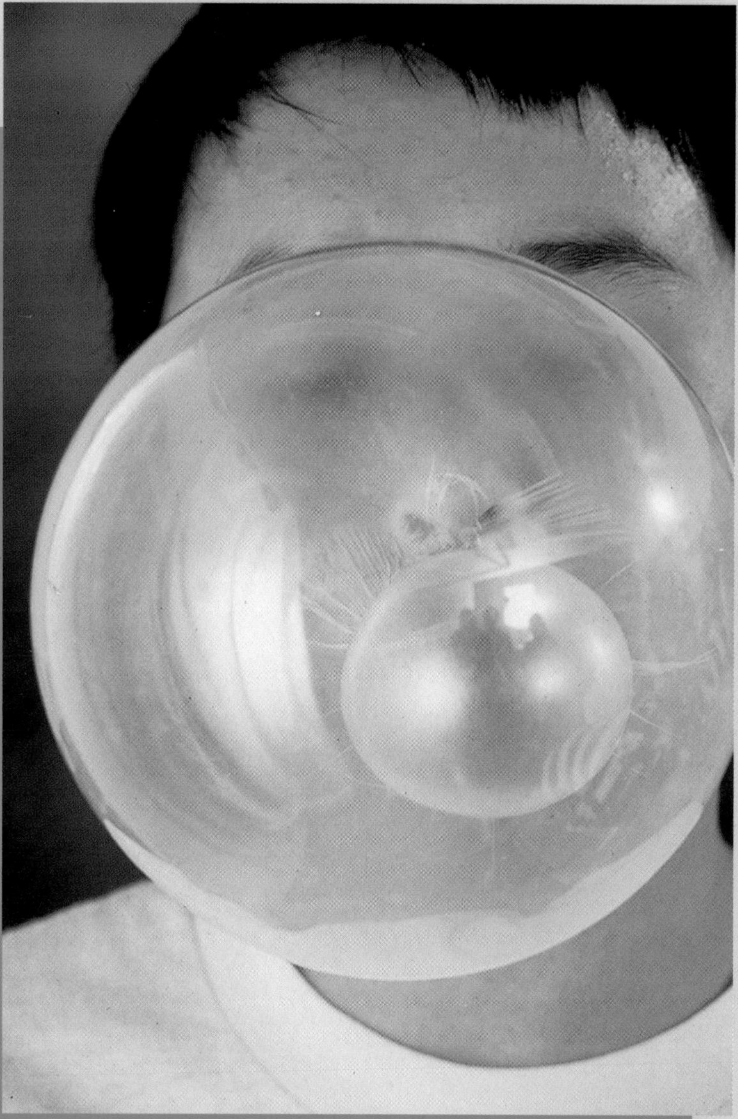

Some kinds of chewing gum come from pigs.

To Find Out More

Here are some additional resources to help you learn more about pigs.

Gibbons, Gail. **Pigs.** Holiday House, 1999.

King-Smith, Dick. **All Pigs are Beautiful.** Candlewick Press, 1993.

Pukite, John. **A Field Guide to Pigs.** Falcon Publishing, 1999.

Radtke, Becky. **Farm Activity Book.** Dover Publications, 1997.

Webster, Charlie. **Farm Animals.** Barron's, 1997.

Wolfman, Judy. **Life on a Pig Farm.** Carolrhoda, 1998.

Organizations and Online Sites

Breeds of Livestock
http://www.ansi.okstate.edu/BREEDS/swine

If you want to see pictures of many different breeds of pigs and descriptions of each, this is the site to visit.

Farm Unit
http://viking.stark.k12.oh.us/~greentown/farmunit.htm

This site from a school in the Midwest has games, information, links to other sites, and a virtual tour of a farm.

Information Dirt Road
http://www.ics.uci.edu/~pazzani/4H/InfoDirt.html

At this site you can get a lot of information on raising different kinds of animals, including pigs.

Kids Farm
http://www.kidsfarm.com

Kids Farm is a lot of fun and educational, too. It is created by people who run a farm in the Colorado Rocky Mountains and brings you real sights and sounds of animals on the farm.

National 4-H Council
http://www.fourhcouncil.edu

This site will tell you about animal clubs and special interest activities for youth across the United States.

Important Words

broth the clear liquid that is made when meat or vegetables are cooking

cornmeal ground corn

factory farm a large farm where a lot of pigs are raised for meat

feeder a young pig that is being raised for meat

litter a group of newborn pigs

shoat a young pig

trough a long, narrow container from which animals can eat or drink

wallow a muddy place where pigs cool off

Index

Meet the Author

Sara Swan Miller has enjoyed working with children all her life, first as a nursery-school teacher, and later as an outdoor environmental educator at the Mohonk Preserve in New Paltz, New York. Now Ms. Miller is a full-time writer. She has written more than thirty books for children, including *Cows*, Chickens, *Goats*, and *Sheep*, in the True Books series.

Photographs ©: Animals Animals: 4 (S. Michael Bisceglie), 2 (Pat Crowe), 16 (Leonard Lee Rue III), 23 (Scott Smith), 32 (Lynn Stone); Bonnie Sue Photography: 28; Bridgeman Art Library International Ltd., London/New York: 7 (MBR124743/Hunting Scene, Gouache and varnish on panel, by Mark Briscoe, Private Collection); Dembinsky Photo Assoc.: 25 (Dusty Perin), 33 (Richard Hamilton Smith); Envision: 40 (B. W. Hoffmann); Liaison Agency, Inc.: 34 (Comedit), 30 (Michael Maiofiss), 26 (Anne Nielsen), 6 (James Schnepf); Lynn M. Stone: 1, 9; Midwestock: 38 (Ben Weddle); New England Stock Photo: 29 (Dusty Perin); North Wind Picture Archives: 8; Peter Arnold Inc.: 35 (James A. Karales); Photo Researchers: cover (Hans Reinhard); Richard Hamilton Smith: 22; Stock Boston: 43 (Frank Siteman); The Image Works: 37 (Jacksonville Journal Courier), 15 (James Marshall); Tony Stone Images: 12 (Renee Lynn), 10 (Andy Sacks); Visuals Unlimited: 17 (D. Cavagnaro), 20 (Jeff Greenberg); Wildlife Collection: 19 (Dietrich Gehring).